AF201584

KALI

Mitali Sengupta

KALI

Many years ago, there lived an asura, a horrible demon called Raktabeej. He wanted to achieve immortality.

'Only Lord Brahma could help me achieve immortality,' he said to himself. Raktabeej decided to meditate to please the Lord.

Lord Brahma was pleased by Raktabeej's devotion. He appeared before him and asked Raktabeej, 'Son, ask what you desire.' Raktabeej asked for immortality. Lord Brahma said, 'I can't give you the gift of immortality.' Raktabeej became remorseful on hearing this. It had been an ardorous task to meditate but he had been a disciplined devotee. Alas! All his efforts had gone wasted.

Lord Brahma continued, 'Son, do not worry. No one will be able to destroy you. Whenever your blood spills on the earth, thousands of your lookalikes will come to life to fight your enemy.' Raktabeej was thrilled to hear this!

Meanwhile, the heavens and earth were being troubled by Raktabeej and the rest of the asuras. He would destroy hermitages and disrupt any good or auspicious work happening anywhere. Kings and gods tried killing him but with his boon it was fast becoming an impossible situation. As a last resort, the gods gathered together and requested Goddess Durga to save them from a terrible end of all life.

Goddess Durga, on hearing news of this new threat and the destruction caused, was annoyed. She decided to create Goddess Kali from her own brows. Kali was a goddess with red eyes and dishevelled hair. She was meant to instil fear and look repulsive to the enemy. She wore a necklace of human heads, and her very presence made one feel the wrath and terror of this maginficient goddess!

As the battle with Raktabeej began, Goddess Kali observed his magical powers. Kali destroyed Raktabeej's army and turned towards Raktabeej. She stretched out her tongue with a war cry and hacked him with her sword. Kali consumed Raktabeej's blood, not letting even one drop fall on earth. The fearsome demon was killed, thus saving mankind and earth. While drinking the blood her complexion turned dark, therefore, her name, Kali – The Dark One.

The goddess, however, did not stop here. She was in a frenzy and in her anger she destroyed anything that came her way. Men and animals fled the scene. Trees were destroyed.

The gods looked worried and they approached Lord Shiva to save the universe from getting destroyed. Lord Shiva assured them. He said, 'Have no worry. I will convince the Goddess to stop her dance of destruction. But first, I must cool her temper.'

Lord Shiva decided to calmly lie down at the scene of destruction. While Goddess Kali busied herself destroying whatever came her way, she failed to see Lord Shiva. Mistaking him for a dead body, she stepped on him.

All of a sudden, Kali recognised Shiva and realising her mistake, put her tongue out as a mark of respect for her husband! Kali was the incarnation of Goddess Durga who was one of the many forms of Parvati, Shiva's wife. At last, Lord Shiva could quieten the goddess' anger. He, thus, saved the earth from further destruction.

Goddess Kali is a fierce form of Goddess Durga. She is dark, representing the moment where time and space have been swallowed! Kali is the three-eyed goddess and she is often depicted as wild and ferocious with dishevelled hair.

She wears a garland of human skulls and she covers her lower body with a string of human hands. She is seen with four hands. In the upper hands, she holds a severed head and a sword. The severed head symbolises the destruction of the human ego. The lower hands are in 'abhaya mudra' meaning that the goddess is blessing her devotees to be fearless, whatever the circumstance or situation.

Her fearlessness is an inspiration and she is particularly worshipped in many parts of North and East India. Goddess Kali represents the supreme energy and is revered by many saints and has a large amount of followers.

Kali is often misunderstood to be the goddess of destruction. In fact, she inspires the regeneration of new things by destroying all that is old and time-worn. She is, therefore, the supreme goddess of Kalyug!

KALI

The demon, Raktabeej has a boon from Brahma which allows him to live forever. With such powers, he sets out to destroy the universe. There is only one way to stop him. It is the entry of the destroyer of all evil, Goddess Kali!

Om Books International

Reprinted in 2024

Corporate & Editorial Office
A-12, Sector 64, Noida 201 301,
Uttar Pradesh, India
Phone: +91 120 477 4100
Email: editorial@ombooks.com
Website: www.ombooksinternational.com

Sales Office
107, Ansari Road, Darya Ganj,
New Delhi 110 002, India
Phone: +91 11 4000 9000
Email: sales@ombooks.com
Website: www.ombooks.com

© Om Books International 2018

ISBN: 978-93-84119-61-4

Printed in India

10 9 8 7 6 5 4 3 2

ALL RIGHTS RESERVED. No part of this book may be reproduced or transmitted in any form by any means, electronic or mechanical, including photocopying and recording, or by any information storage and retrieval system, except as may be expressly permitted in writing by the publisher.

ISBN 978-93-84119-61-4 US $ 3.99 £ 3.50
9 789384 119614
www.ombooksinternational.com 0012500

eBOOK available

ombooksinternationalofficial ombooksinternational ombooksdelhi